AF255815

Oxford Street

Oxford Street

Poetry in the Psychology of Childhood
Volume 1

David C. Bellusci

RESOURCE *Publications* · Eugene, Oregon

OXFORD STREET
Poetry in the Psychology of Childhood, Volume 1

Resource Publications
An Imprint of Wipf and Stock Publishers
199 W. 8th Ave., Suite 3
Eugene, OR 97401

www.wipfandstock.com

PAPERBACK ISBN: 978-1-6667-6346-1
HARDCOVER ISBN: 978-1-6667-6347-8
EBOOK ISBN: 978-1-6667-6348-5

02/21/23

To the memory of my mother and my father

*And Kronos swallowed them all down as soon as each
Issued from Rhea's holy womb onto her knees,
With the intent that only he among the proud Ouranians
Should hold the title of King among the Immortals.*

Theogony (463–466)

Contents

Preface

In this collection of poems, the child Apollo represents the main character among the Greek gods; the names and relations resemble Hesiod's *Theogany*. The poems shift to Oxford Street signifying the dynamics of family relations transferred onto the psyche of a child and what is stored in the unconscious.

Apollo is the son of Hestia and Zeus. Apollo's half-brother, Dionysios, and his sister, Demeter, are the issue of Hera and Zeus. Kronos is Zeus's father. Apollo also has several aunts and uncles, brothers and sisters of his father and his father's consort, Hera.

The family relations, ties between gods and goddesses across generations, shapes Apollo's understanding of himself as he follows what appears to be the direction of his father Zeus, under the guidance of his mother, Hestia.

On Oxford Street the experience of childhood and the desire for independence, reflects the energetic child learning about relations and "overcoming" the oppressiveness of conflict and competing authority—omnipresent and omniscient.

The underlying archaeology is found in Greek mythology. With the events on Oxford Street, the growing stages, relational development, internal tension, the poetry is framed to include the classical schools of psychology.

Acknowledgments

I am grateful to my poetry mentors at the University of Nebraska, in particular, Allison Adelle Hedge Coke, Teri Grimm and Lee Ann Roripaugh. I am indebted to them as professors, writers, and artists.

The late Pier Giorgio Di Cicco has been a source of inspiration for me. I first met Pier Giorgio on St. Michael's campus at the University of Toronto in 2004; his words of encouragement have kept me writing.

Francesca L'Orfano, the late visual artist and videographer, reminded me that art "is meant to be communicated." Our many conversations on culture and creativity, art and poetry, led me towards conferences, workshops, and publishing. I am grateful to Rosanna Battigelli for her energy and writing, her encouraging comments, but especially her friendship.

In terms of the psycho-therapeutic influences in my writing I have been blessed with the friendship of Rev. Ajith Varghese working in mental health. I am grateful to Professor John Morgan who provided me with a pastoral angle to psychotherapy. I also wish to thank Dr. Hanna Pytlak who listened to me since I first visited her office.

FAMILY OF GODS

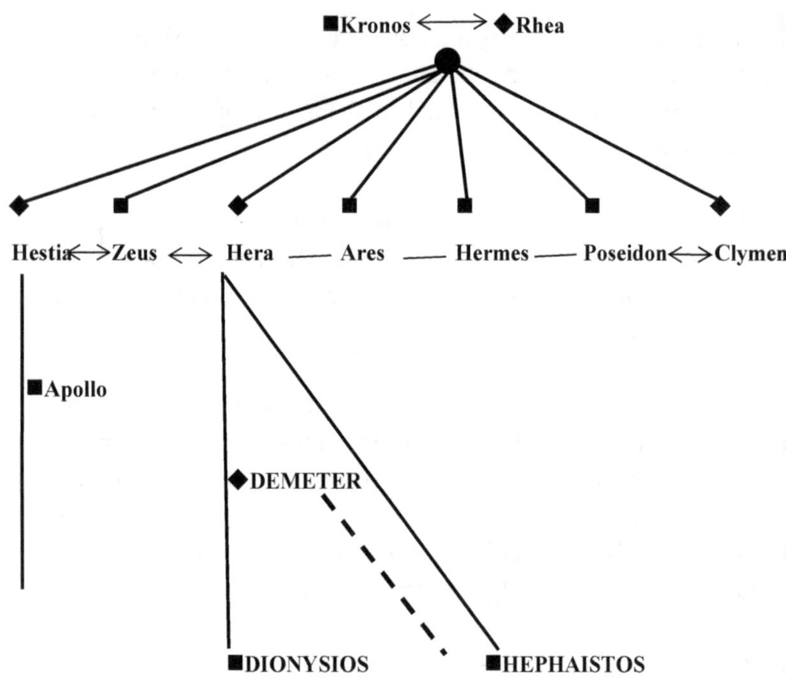

Statue of a Mother Breastfeeding

Peasant woman,
head scarf, vibrant clothes,
she sits in a chair
holds her baby, focused
on his lips sucking
her breast.

Intimate smile.

Baby's eyes set on his mother.

Her hands on her breast ensures her boy
is satisfied with her milk.

Gratified. Peace.

Woman captures maternity,
in her rosy cheeks, full breasts,
healthy hips.

Is it the woman or child
who delights in this ceramic
of natural attachment?

Baby breastfed.
Breastfeeding Mother.

The statue remained on my mother's
dresser.

Oxford Street

Two-story stucco or Craftsman homes,
decorated front gables. Banisters
hide porches, brown or turquoise
or gray. Staircases roll down the center.
Neighbors
Croatians and Italians,
family from Germany own the toys,
and the Japanese home
at the corner
boasts the only colour television.
We peek through the windows
to watch cartoons.
Mamma relies on
the front porch to yell out our names
for supper. We could hear
from the playground, the next block.
Papa uses the garage as a mechanic's workshop
where he works in the day,
or weekends after his nightshift.
I notice mamma
from the back alley with shopping
bags making her way home from work.
It seems like a one hour walk from my Grade One class
or three quarters of an hour from mamma's shop where I stop
after school. But my sister tells me
not even ten minutes
from our school to Oxford Street.

Two-Story House

        We all sleep
on the second story.
    I feel secure on the top floor:
from our bedroom window daylight
pours
      as I face the mountains north.
It looks onto the narrow street
and our neighbors' homes.
Small white room for the toilet;
spacious bathroom contains
a white sink and tub.
    I observe
papa shave as the lather on his blade
accumulates with each stroke until
he rinses the razor under the running water.
Occupants change, family, friends
tenants shifting
        rented space and rooms
        occupied-dis-occupied.
        Each of us visits
the kitchen in intervals
where mamma cooks. The big window
faces the garage where papa repairs cars.
    I dreaded the basement floor
    where I seldom went.
    Dark deep below I felt alone
and threatened by the underworld of beasts.

Lurking

Thoughts of Freud,
his dream analysis, symbols,
and interpretation.
Darkness descends frightfully
into the depth of a basement
—a killer rat appears,
signifies "being dead":[1]
mortal danger.
Natural fear.
Innate. A child without being taught
understands the unintelligible
a void of Unknown
and non-visible.
The Lurking.
Absence of light,
leaves an underworld of beings
free to roam.

1. Freud, *Psychoanalysis*, 103.

Nightmare Rat

My nighttime sleep leads me
to the basement door
down the first flight of stairs
facing the wall. The stairs creak in the dark.
I imagine someone hides
behind the stairs and grabs
my bare feet.
I continue down the stairs
to the second flight facing the basement,
open area of total darkness.
A rat jumps out.
Its head filling
the basement and huge eyes staring
directly at me. I turn around
and run back up the stairs. The rat shuffles
behind me. The first flight.
The second flight.
I slam the door shut . . .

Tarturos

Appearance of Darkness
looms in his creepy activity,
breathing
a child's deep sleep—and nightmare.
This god seeks
to cover me
as if on a mission—sent by whom?
I feel the dark blanket.
Heavy.
But its thickness unable to cover me.
The rat springs out
a frightful presence,
trying to bite me with its poison
of deadly toxins.
Power beyond my own
childish fear flings me
to the first story:
       door leads to light
I only need to open
—and shut
to keep the rat out.

Jungian Shadows

Descent into darkness, black
pit so it feels, where sweaty
silent breathing, uneven steps,
whisper my presence==
joined by unknown company==
eyes hidden behind the walls
lock into secrecy.
My pyjamas drag at my feet,
my white undershirt hangs.
Dark mahogany panels, bare.
I dwell in fear. As if tied==
unable to loosen my body,
I stand alone in an abyss
that devours my being. Only one
large window to exit==
or someone to enter.
In blackness as fear looms thick
I remain still.

Papa in the Morning

In the dark bedroom
encased in high walls
half asleep
awake to sounds and rhythm:
mama breathes.
Withdrawn into her world
of dreams forgetting
to bring me with her.
Darkness surrounds me. Afraid.
For mamma . . . for myself . . .
Click of the key tricks my ears.
Which door? Papa?
Mamma undisturbed.
My heart beats—thumps.
I feel my ears as if pressing
against the hard door.
I recognize papa's steps closer
comforted by his ritual:
door—staircase—kitchen.
Still,
thickness black draped
in heavy cotton,
calm covers me, and dawn sleep.

Fuzzy Feeling

Secure, comforted,
reassured presence, rhythms
of love without words,
child feels bodily warmth,
snore and heavy breathing,
sounds recognized:
familiar repetition
creates trust,
protection predicted,
sounds known.
Assurance and affirmation,
Abraham Maslow identifies,
child grows healthy, primary
needs fulfilled:
loved and lovable.[1]
Music of breathy presence
meaning without syllables
warmth suffices for a child
to sleep and dream.

1. Maslow, *Psychology of Being,* 117–18.

Morning Fire

Papa secure in his wooden chair
moves forward close to the fire,
throws in wood.
His face brightens
with each hard dry piece. The hiss
and crackle of licking flames
heats the basement, creates light.
Papa's face shines.
Only on weekends when papa
stays home to work in the garage,
and when I don't have school,
I sneak downstairs
to the illuminated walls and floor
to join papa in silence.
With the poker he shifts the wood
to create more heat, brighter light,
as I drink the warmth
—darkness dispelled.

Zeus in Battle

He senses a plot
     his brother, Poseidon,
     Hera's brothers, Ares and Hermes,
     his father, Kronos . . .
Zeus laments:
he lacks warriors; he cries, *war!*
     without fighters.
Kronos bellows:
     Zeus bolts without thunder,
     what kind of god is he?
Hera's brothers ignore Zeus.
But the sweet hisses of Poseidon, Zeus trusts:
     his brother possesses serpentine knowledge
     (though Poseidon finds Hestia intolerable)
     prompted by Poseidon's consort, Clymene
     and offers a solid alliance.
Late at night when Artemis appears
his daughter showers
moonlight to soothe Zeus,
but instead anger builds.
Zeus seeks a goat to take on his wrath.
Hestia's son, Young Apollo, stands in his path,
saliva dripping
from Zeus' rough purple lips.
Hestia takes charge, commands Apollo:
"Move out of your father's way!"

Apollo obeys his mother;
exits the home if only temporarily.
Following his mother's instructions,
allows the anger of Zeus to subside.

Apollo runs . . .
        into frosty fields . . .

Knitting Machine

Past the first story entrance,
mamma knits every evening
    in the small dining area.
Italian knitting machine transported
by her father across the Atlantic
    occupies half the dining room space.
After mamma's work, after dinner,
sitting on the floor—on an angle,
I observe in wonder:
    mamma slides back and forth
    the plastic arm pulling
    yellow yarn
    transforming a seamless fabric.
She holds up her rectangular creation.
    displays the piece.
My hands folded I smile at mamma's
reconfigured fibers, like play.

Erickson's Work and Play

Play intermingles
mountain climb
ocean dive—
    early morning fishing
    chopping firewood.
Neither fear, nor hope for the outcome
conditions.[1]
Play pushes away anxiety:
    play is fun.
Neither necessity nor compulsion
belong to play.
Play makes me human:
    beyond drives
    beyond instincts
    play transcends.
God's play.
Erikson admits
play
eludes definition:
    adult's work; child's play.

---

1. Erikson, *Childhood and Society*, 191.

Golden Fleece

Hera miraculously obtains
soft layers
from the gold lamb stretching
across the rugged hills
of Thessaly.
I accompany her to "dog's head."
Ancient rocks paint
words of mystery.
Shorn fleece scatters
into a sculpture. Hera explains,
Covers for a young man,
Hephaistos, her daughter's betrothed.
Demeter interjects:
    —Why does Hephaistos
need the fleece?
    —I cannot say. Your father
knows nothing. Nor must you reveal
anything to Zeus.

Hera's secret.

First-Floor Dining Table

Saturday afternoon, I enter
first floor doors entertained by
dining table garden.
Gold floral corners disappear
under embroidered white cover
of grapes and oranges.
Window frames
cotton curtains
unveil porcelain figures on the ledge.
Mamma's priceless treasures,
broken and glued.
I stood in wonder, captured
by the table's display:
genovese salami,
black forest ham, prosciutto,
parmesan cheese, olives,
fresh loaf of french bread,
canned tuna fish—in oil.
Light pours into the kitchen
on the golden harvest.

Glued figurines process
in their pastel shades of green and blue.

Constellation

Adler considers the family
constellation, indicative—last born:
siblings; rivals.[1]
Need to prove to adults
in child's grownup world.
All dominate:
father—mother—brother.
Authority exercised over power-less-ness.
How does the last born
psychologically survive.
Myth: overprotected spoiled child.

Warmth escapes the last born.
Too late?
Approval. Acceptance. Belonging.
    —not just appendage:
    waits—withdrawn—in silence.
Youngest lacks
experience and knowledge,
does not know—cannot be trusted.
Questioned:
    two extremes:
    high achiever—insecure:
    neurosis minorae.

1. Adler, *Human Nature,* 149–52.

Kitchen Boils

Big sink in front of me, small fridge
on the left, cupboards above,
window with frames, stove to the right,
enough space for mamma and papa,
and me, quietly standing to observe.
I feel the after work tension;
mamma needs space to cook,
papa present, to help or enquire, or advise.
The procedure I follow: pasta poured
into boiling water on the stove,
after a few minutes, cooked,
steaming hot, pasta poured into the strainer.
I inhale the hot vapors
rising from the steel,
pasta cooked right, heated sink.
Process a matter of minutes,
mamma focused: rhythm
of pasta, pot, sink, strainer.
I notice mamma place the huge pot
of boiling water between counter and stove,
balance on an angle.
She turns to pour the pasta.
Papa in the kitchen, space tight,
pot hit. Like a caldron, boiling water
splashes
on mamma's legs
in front of me.

I hear mamma scream.

Hephaistos' Proposal

Delphic goddesses greets mother.

Hephaistos stands not far
with the Nereids
messaged in the falls
of bubbling waters.

Mother consults the Delphic oracle.

Turns to me and speaks
of Artemis.

Hot salty substance pours from rocks

    scorches mother

    she releases a deadly shrill

      caught by Hephaistos.

Mother moans
in agony or confusion . . .

She questions Hephaistos'
deepest desires.

Hephaistos pleads to Hera her consent:

to permit Artemis as his bride.

Surprising wish:

Artemis was destined for Delphi.

Unraveling *Fate*

    Pleasure or pain—
    pursuit and avoidance
life does not belong to either.
Rather, "to see meaning in life,"
Viktor Frankl's existential claim:[1]
life has purpose . . .
    cooking dinner
    working in a garage pit
    rearing a child
exhausted—burned—scalded
self-offering, to suffer—to sacrifice
    not the human goal
    but meaningfulness extracted
    from a human act.
Wedded gods
Oracle virgin
destined for meaning.
Created for happiness, like the gods?
Indeed, but as mortals,
    fragile and finite,
    suffering encounters the depth
    of meaning.

1. Frankl, *Man's Search*, 108–9.

Mamma's Chevrolet

On Oxford Street,
automobile hugs the curb,
parked
opposite our two-story
home.

Black shiny hair, she smiles,
leans
against her Chevrolet
in her offwhite dress,

photo with us.

    Mamma—
the only woman
in our neighborhood
who knows how to drive.

Summer afternoon,
photo faces west,
our house south of the mountains.

Empty block,
except green grass, picket fences
and mamma's Chevrolet.

Papa taught her to drive.

Riding Pegasus

Pegasus cries out Hestia's name . . .
white horse spreads its wings
mother arrives to find her place
at my side.
Majestic winged horse flies
into white clouds, falling angel
hair.
Mother points below
to temples,
Athens, Delphi, Olympus,
home of brother gods and sister goddesses;
stories of Olympians and Titans.
She names them all . . .
I cannot remember.
Earlier, Demeter and Hephaistos
revealed their divine powers
over deer and grapes.
I discover the meaning of Athena's owl,
and the parthenogenic birth
of the first gods.

Mother Bonds

Youngest child, always the "baby"
    unlike the firstborn—dethroned,
    attention shared with rivals.[1]

Mother,
    provides experience of love:
        embracing arms, satisfying milk
        smile reassures
transforms into psycho-affectivity
    never disappears—
            skill . . . knowledge . . . wisdom,
            she directs
            her child's potentialities—growth.

Father's dedication, a good man,
    to wife . . . child . . . society.

All await the Complex resolution,

      thus, speaks Freud.

---

1. Adler, *Individual Psychology*, 372–74.

Papa's Garage

The narrow lane behind Oxford Street
stood a row of garages
in pastel shades,
          ours turquoise.

Papa works all night
     during his time off
     the day
     weekends
     in the garage.
Papa sleeps in the morning.

Cars parked as if resting,
expecting to be serviced.
Greasy mechanic tools, dark green
shelves, oily cement floor
surround me,
and the pit
below,
where papa hides beneath cars
in his dark blue uniform.

The pit scares me.
Anxious. As if a car
crushes papa.

I bend over from the side to observe;
my thoughts focused
on the weight of the car
and papa's fragile body.
His hands smeared in grease.

I fear his fall

      in the dark.

Invisible Darkness

At times Zeus disappears

into the dark, battles fought:

Tycon, even Tartarus.

Father's withdrawal into the abyss
frightens me

not knowing his whereabouts
or return.

He says nothing. . .

Wars ongoing, as if father
returns only to depart

late at night.

Never certain of his fate—

father displays anger and rage;

mother explains the wars and darkness
afflict father.

I never understood; I only fear
the empty dwelling.

Finding Archaic Man

Confronting invisible forces
armed for war,

archers shoot arrows, escape
slaughter.

Visible battles we fight—perceive
a deadly threat.

Rational nature held prisoner—
empirical—verifiable—quantifiable.

Deadly unmeasurable poses no
danger.

Idea of an unseen power we "resent";
cast aside suggestions.[1]

Eighteenth century Reason means
constructing a world we control.

Intelligible.

As if we transcend the invisible—

arbitrary forces, ourselves.

1. Jung, *Modern Man*, 130.

Papa at Dinner

Dining table, oval-shaped,
gold branches on white marble base.

Papa occupies the seat up front,
door behind him,
leads to the patio.

Darkness hurries across the window,
panes chiselled winter black.
Thickness of moisture, heavy;
bodies occupy positioned chairs.

Dinner knives cut tension
an immanent storm.

Sudden frightful roar . . .

uncertain trigger,

I observe myself stop
startled in my red scooter
to examine papa in his white undershirt
make gestures while he speaks
forgets the food in front of him.

Voice built up; power of thunder.

Mamma puts on my jacket,

sends me outside . . . 31

Child Locked in Fear

Fear reflects my powerlessness
over the outer world;

how did that child respond?

Safety—security.

        What . . . ?

Immanent danger—instincts:[1]

self-preservation to follow human
nature.

Where . . . ?

    I withdraw to a hidden haven.

Same cloudless blue sky
    I navigate to a place of calm.

Child intuits the vulnerable condition:
helplessness.

---

1. Freud, *Psychoanalysis*, 343.

To escape intense reactions,
or to suffocate in anxiety

when I fear the trembling state

of mamma.

Friday Night Movies with Papa

When warm Spring evenings wrap us,
from Oxford Street papa brings me
to the theater on that busy intersection.

I claim my maroon seat beside him.

My eyes focus:
a gigantic screen
      bulging muscles
      of boulder breaking Hercules,
      courage embodied.
Papa spits
to defend Herculean truths.
My attention switches
from Hercules to papa. I stare
      then glance
      at our Herculean hero.

We return to Oxford Street in the dark.
Tired I fall asleep in his arms
all the way home . . .

Analyzing Mythical Narratives

Paint brushes probe
    the petrified unconscious
    strata of solid rock
    images of myth
        battles triggered.[1]
Deeper analysis blue zone
    untouched/untouchable.
    Shielded.
        Affectionate love
        makes connections:
knowledge dreams
Truth.
        Co-related—
            Goodness.
            Some include Beauty.

---

1. Maslow, *Psychology of Being,* 70, 138.

Vested Mystery

Rows of coats, dark jackets, solid tone dresses
block my view. On my toes I struggle
to pierce through any opening . . .
gazing between necks, tall bodies
enduring struggle.

     What are they staring at?

  words in unison
  postures change in rhythm
  everybody grasps
     except me.

Finally, I turn to mamma,
    What are they doing?"
  I observe men in ritual performance,
   distinct white robes.
Her head bows slightly towards me
whispers, behind her black veiled hat
eyes secretly covered:
    It's a sacrifice.

Apollo at Delphi

Accompanying Hestia to Delphi, I
take my place
beside mother.
Oracle comprised of Olympian goddesses,
Temple Virgins, who receive
a sacrificial bull from the humans
since Prometheus stole the light:
    Bidding—
        Favors
        Forgiveness
    Offering—
        Worship
        Thanksgiving
I visited the Holy Temple
once before with Zeus. Father
spilling blood remains in my memory.
I witness the slaughter again;
perhaps I might grasp
why sacrifice pleases the gods.

Signs of Gods

By our nature we profess—
or repress
signs of Transcendence.
Demands for a visible God:
sensory—empirical—primitive epistemology.

David Hume fails to seize
non-material—only his constructed
response to primitive needs.

Substance, angels, God,
escape sense categories.
    Empiricist's shallow conclusions
based on defective premises.

But intelligence capable of Truth.

Medieval metaphysics contested:
        Age of Light.
Validity of negation resurfaces—
five centuries later.
Linguistics and psychology revive
scholastic claims:
    "It is possible in language to
    arrive at truth—one truth."[1]

---

1. Frankl, *Will to Meaning,* 117.

Mortals at the Crossroads

In Corinth mortals performed
the tragedy of Oedipus, "swollen-feet"
chained as a child.
Oracles at Delphi
tell the truth. Cithaeron mountains offer
comfort except the sphinx at Thebes
—his riddles. Thebes anoints brutal
wounds of the gods.
Murderous affair at the crossroads.
Thebans bowed
before Oedipus and Jocasta
until the gods inflicted
a plague upon citizens, animals, and crops.
Greek chorus called—
gods to intervene:
Athena, Artemis, Zeus. Even Apollo.
Ungodly humans; gods too human.

. . . seeking a way out.

Daffodils and Bumblebees[1]

In our Croatian neighbor's garden
a widow plants
rows of marigold in her corner home.
Husband died fishing the Adriatic.
She waters and sprinkles in summer;
cold and damp disappear.

But I prefer yellow dandelions spilled across our
front yard with tall green weeds
I can hide in.

Papa fixes cars in his garage pit; works on a blue
Buick. I am scared he'll get crushed. My brother
looks greasy helping—both smell oily.

Opposite side of our block, couple unmarried, one
divorced, the other—rumors, French-Canadian.
Her sons—his sons, we play. We share roast beef,
potatoes with buns and butter
at their home.

My buddy from next door knocks me
to the ground and gobs on my face. Others pin me
down. Friends with the Howard's, I figured
I am not supposed to.

1. A version of this poem was read at the Association of Italian-Canadian Writers (Winnipeg, MB, September 27–29, 2018).

Me and my sister hear him get whipped
on the weekends by his father when their
housekeeper leaves. We even walk to his mother's
new suite. A timid woman. He screams so loud my
sister slams shut the window. A ritual. We played
cowboys together—until the Howard's arrived.

A pretty girl lives up the block
two years older than me; I think she just turned ten.
She sneaks into bed, and so do I,
when nobody notices. We laugh, lying beside each
other, telling funny stories.

I can still feel his warm gob on my face.

Boeotian Hills

Sheep graze in sunlight.
Grass bright green layers
whisper.
White fur deep as snow,
winter garment.

Father tells me yellow flowers spurt;
choke the crops.
Carpet of deceiving gold stretches
across the fields.

Tender dizziness.

Gods fought on these hills;
the damp smell of earth testifies.

Father calls it, "Battle of Hera":

    his consorts and offspring
    driven
    by the goddess of motherhood.

Summer Lemonade

We set the chipped . . . turquoise table,

on the sidewalk
in front of our house.

Not sure about neighbors
strolling past to finish our jug
            . . . of lemonade.

Glasses—three sizes:

    SMALL—ten cents!
    MEDIUM—fifteen cents!
    LARGE—twenty-five cents!

Prices visibly marked
for Oxford Street passersby.

    My job, shout: "Lemonade!"

. . . the jug finished with one last
large glass sold to the man wearing
a cowboy hat.

He chugged the drink, sipped the pulp.

I'm not sure
if we rinsed the glasses.

Neighborhood Interventions

Classroom experience of cooperation
they say.[1]

On Oxford Street our neighbors
unite—
we support each other
with friendly visits.

When Bobby was struck by a car, mamma ran to fetch
a blanket
to keep him warm...

We stood around Bobby and observed
mamma cautiously place the quilted blanket over him
until we heard the ambulance
with red sirens arrive, stop at the spot
where Bobby lay
under colorful quilt patches.

After he returned from the hospital
Bobby tricked me into trading my rifle
that shot loud and hard,
for his plastic pistol—which I regret.

On Oxford Street in the front lawn,
we have our fights—they outnumber me
and win.

1. Adler, *Individual Psychology*, 402–3.

Mother's Warning

Athena joins the nereids

Olympian splashes

in the Aegean.

Dawn sun bounces
off waves, dark depths,
    octopus arms suckered, cold fingers
    of dark green slime trickle.

I rise to the surface, like a triton;
corals stretch
transformed butterflies in the sand.

Sounds of exhausted laughter not far,

familiar voices . . . Athena

escapes

to join them in Thessaly's fields.
Orchards of lemons trees,
afternoon scent.

Sirens from the sea, pierce,
as if next to me.

But I remember mother say,
	not to turn around . . .

Car Shock

Her body folded,
beneath the watermill painting,
cries interject dinner:
syllables stretched by shrills, screams,
words broken. I struggle to make
sense of sounds.
On a breezy Spring afternoon,
mechanical failure . . . her car . . . on a hill.
Phone call to her younger brother:
he test drives the vehicle—downhill.
Brakes fail.
Sharp turn.
Steel death trap
        flips over...and over...

Mamma takes home her trembling
body,
convulsions of an engine
and her brother's deadly
        stop.

Preparing for Battle

Hera keeps her distance
from the stone quarry.

My eyes focus on Hephaistos
smiting iron,
bellows create gold and red glow
like volcanic lava
pouring from Methana.

Heavy iron sword smitten for Ares in defense
of the Olympians.

Whether clumsy or foolish
but without intention
Hephaistos hits Ares
when the smiting hammer strikes the iron,
and the anvil sent the burning sword flying.

Ares falls
on the weapon's impact;
and Hera shocked by his collapse
as if a dead god
shuts her eyes horrified.

My eyes shift,
no longer Hephaistos or Ares,
but to Hera's grief.

Child's Silence

Childhood: feels powerless:
      unalterable injustice
           reality disturbs.
Human vulnerability,
innocence absorbs
        triangle of emotions //
Life sets determined goal:
transcend fragile tragedy
        witness to triumph.[1]
Adult integrates meaning
        makes sense of events
[attempts]
        to transform unavoidable
        suffering,

    endurance, courage
        willing survivor.

---

1. Frankl, *Man's Search*, 112.

Yelling Our Names

Playing on the shadeless school ground,
late afternoon sun warms the wind
on Oxford Street.
Baseball in summer heat
screams of *strike!*—or *run!*
My sister—older—faster, shouts
like others on the block
until we hear
our names called:
    mamma cries out
      from the balcony edge
        faces the school.
Banister shields mamma's legs
        her name always first . . .
        prolonged *aaaaa*
            then mine . . . prolonged *eeeee.*
The game ends right there for us
winners unknown
we return home
mamma waits to serve us pasta
two minutes up Oxford Street.

Prohibited Music

Mother tells me
to avoid the sirens, and not to listen
to their voices . . . lyrics . . . or music.

Sirens produce a hypnotic spell.

Once I fell into a trance.

I lost control of my senses and surroundings.

Mother warns me—believes
I am too young to understand their sweet
melodies and manoeuvres.

I run under the lemon
orchards the citric scent filling my
my pores. I taste the fruit
with my skin as if my legs and hands
and chest and head possess buds.

But the scent
turns into sharp hums
like a child's cry. And I feel my body pulled
by sweet screeches.

The waves of the Aegean splash against
rocks—my boyhood flesh.

Sirens pierce . . .

I am torn by mother.

Time to Play

Games open the green paths
to the future:
running from base to post,
aim to advance—excel.[1]
For the team we lick our sweat
run after our screams
wipe our noses on sleeves.
Thirst wags its finger—we ignore,
teammates play for victory.
Afternoon sun burns my body,
in-built energy.
    Batter.
        Runner.
Neighbors from Oxford Street,
boys my age, girls,
my sister's friends, we bounce on summer
sand. Connectedness with the block—
to win!
Honor fulfilled
for sweaty faces on each side.
Strike. Strike. Strike.
      My soul struck.

---

1. Adler, *Human Nature*, 48.

At the Dinner Table

Thickness of vapors
    sweaty eyebrows
    depends on a trigger word:
        in-laws—he and she,
    names of streets
    a piece of property, East Second Ave.
        failed investment
        or missed?
His leveled tone
emphatic syllables stretch
my eyes shift, ears wrapped
      —like mamma's apron.
I tighten stiff in my chair
cold food
on the white brim plate.
Green peas mushy, meat too veiny
to swallow.

I withdraw into silence.

Banqueting with Zeus

He lands in front of us, legs bent
on the mosaic marble floor.
Table cloths of white linen
—rose petals strewn off the center.
  We feel the storm
    velvet curtains upset
    red drops fall
    darkness.
Familiar faces evaporate.
Loud deep voice fills
the large octagonal room
    with falling pitch.
  Guilt and fear strike at me.
  Uncertain why.
Mother remains silent, composed,
her resolute figure unchanged.
No other voices heard. Only my
heart-beat almost too loud.
I pray for calm.

He disappears—hiding—

Past Perceptions

We retain traces of perception
of the external world—
our surroundings—[1]

Photograph creates memory;
not stored perceptions.

A child recognizes: prominence—
early patterns identified
certainly predictable.

Sensory data does not correspond
to the actual world:
Loud. Rude. Boorish.

My soul is tied
to a child's recollection of images:

      archeology
      excavations.

1. Adler, *Human Nature*, 48.

Painting of a Waterwheel

Painting in the dining room, hangs
framed on cream wall.
Distant theme—crashes.
The water wheel cools me
blue skies raise me
to infinity
and dark oak conveys home,
somewhere . . .
standing alone
solid paddles spin.

Ash trees secure the flow, secret medicine.
Forgotten country.
Far. Nobody. Soulless.
I hear only water,
motion of blades—spin
rhythmic—endless.
I lie stretched out
with green trees, shaded spectator,
breezy water scented shelter.

Cool moss caresses my skin.

Corinthian Disk

We descended in the Peloponnese,
father and I.

He explained the working of the wheel—
human inventions
that resemble the Divine.

Father points to the wood wheel paddles
driven by water—
rotations.

Motions carry water. Circular source.
One
perfect unity
no beginning no end.

With enough determined force
paddle pushes, water gushes
endless, like the gods.
I know the nereids, their god Nereus
in charge.

I turn to father, and hear
the strength of Zeus

Finding Art

Paint layers blur blue greens:
awe-created disks and dials
expected/imposed:[1]
         others reconfigure
basis of judging—desire imprinted
silent drops rhythmic
—or textures secretly suggested
           as if free
actions read
individual's
social interest penetrates
truth in love embraced—the other—

fragments of bone, hidden tooth,
chipped flakes
    withdrawal from the world
    of humanity
—but painted:
sages instruct/inspire
    solitude undefined
    —thought provoked;
    heart beats.

1. Adler, *Individual Psychology*, 449.

Red Rover . . .

==we call==Johnny over==
Two parallel chains mixed
boys and girls
in the front yard—neighbor's house
—anyone's. Two chains of at least ten
hands==tightly==held.
Yellow daffodils stuck to stucco
wall brightens the path.
Boys' hand squeeze==unbreakable.
Girls', gentle==softer==easier.
I secretly aim==
jolt across the thick grass
for the two sisters==I break through.
I join the chain==between==them,
my friend my age, her sister, older.
Feeling of warm hands on either side,
secures me.
Red Rover==Red Rover==we==call==
Now to keep the next kid
from smashing
through our hands==I hold tight
eyes search . . .

Unplayful Gods

Children of the gods never play:
brothers battle; sisters weep;
mothers jealous; fathers threaten.

Strategies planned on Olympus
shift to Thessaly.

Endless anger of Zeus
rivals Kronos.

Clymene's ruthless stabs.

Zeus rescues Poseidon—
only to become the sea serpent's victim.
Then Zeus grieves for Poseidon,
forgets mother,
devastated.

No contemplation or leisure or play.

The marble Roman slab,
my cold chair. I gaze into the fields
where their tragedies repeat . . .

Fragile Play

Sensation swims
heart tickles, blood warms.
Preadolescent security, experienced
satisfaction
nature's capacities.[1]
Juvenile's ladder: parallel—steps.
Difference/Resemblance.
Similar justifies
disSimilar.
Eyes smile, hands kiss,
affection facilitated by her love.
My reality extends—deepens—
encounter with her
within.
Love directs my gaze:
determined direction
illuminated.
I feel human. Search begins . . .

1. Sullivan, *Modern Psychiatry,* 42–43.

Cousin's Farewell

New colors added to our Oxford house
her shiny black hair—long, red lip stick—
deep mascara eyelashes.
She studies English while employed
in a downtown factory.

Teasing her as if my older sister,
I broadcast my new vocabulary
my cousin my teacher:
stupid, I blurt with a smirk.
Enough! She cracks like lightening,
bolts the family chatter.
I poke at my plate.
Charge of silence contains
her electricity.

Weeks later we accompany my cousin to the train
station. I observe her board.
Mamma inquires if I wish to join my cousin.
She disappears behind closing doors
into her cabin. Lowered window.

I wave to the vanishing train.

Siren's Warning

I approach the sirens—*that one.*

Something mother forbade.

As the ship passes the rocks
on the Aegean shores
Corinth at a distance
my ears plugged
I take notice of her. I return
early morning
the blue waves welcome me
crashing against the rocks.

She emerges. My fingers in my ears,
my urge to be closer—I feel her
hypnotic pull—to sleep at her side
on the remote rocks.

Siren's sudden shrill hits me like
a ship's oar: I fall out of fear.

Empathy and Childhood

We experience our feelings
—sensitivity—fear.

Seek assurance. Not betrayal.

We cannot deny
the feelings of another.[1]
And so, relations
can be "lived"—feelings we own: "real."

And yet . . . our expressions
others interpret,
respond—react—reject.
Child conveys in subtle jokes
an inner quest . . .
       shut // down
          // out
          // off

1. Rogers, *Becoming a Person*, 318.

Wrecked Ship

On the floor upstairs of our Oxford Street
home, a rented room to a mother and son,
I heard.
His mother offered us a tour of the refurbished
room and sailing ships.
My age, he displays his built boats
made from popsicle sticks.
When the two leave the house
and nobody remains at home,
secretly,
I slip upstairs; I revisit our rented
space.
I scan the area,
eyeing the ships. At work I disassemble
the most intricate details,
stick by stick unstuck.
I delight in my deconstructive voyage . . .
Early evening exasperated
shrieks expelled, traumatized boy,
child reacts to sticks scattered . . .
Mamma upset with my breaking an entry
of a tenant's room, the rod is not spared
to ensure *I* felt the boy's pain.

Satisfied he observes
mamma's measured justice.

Mortal Games

I never understood: mortals
lack divine power and knowledge
while these creatures believe they possess both.

Their ships, Spartans, Athenians,
as if mighty gods!

Wrath struck Zeus, he charged;
embodied humans
a confused lot living in darkness
escape the light
blamed by mortals and gods.

Impeded they grasp little, poor vision,
real dimwits.
Naval strategies to destroy,
imitate divine power.

I am . . . what are you, fragile mortal?
You believe to be a god,
sharing with gods the sublime and vicious.
Holy. Deadly.
Sails set. Ships approach.
Prepare for war.

Interpreting Childplay

Reflecting on Erikson, a mother
interprets her son's
destructive ## state.[1]
Toy belongs to a stranger,
child feels he must destroy it ##
The pleasure taken##
in the act##
after the mother and child
spend hours
putting pieces together.
He feels he needs to wreck ##
in a room ## in secret ##
The aggressive## boy
does not construct.
His pleasure emptied of power,
domination focussed##
Clearly stronger, the other weak.
Child's play—to master ##reality.

1. Erikson, *Childhood and Society*, 197.

Falling Christmas Tree

Pine tree, green scented needles
layered branches, six feet decorated.
Grandma's bubbling oil lights,
red Santa Claus, angel hair and icicles,
ornaments we fix
in night time pajamas—
snowflakes signal presents, count to dawn.

Trunk never fit into the metal base,
stands slightly angled.
Heart beats hard, try to catch . . .
falling tree.

My sister picks up decorations.
I examine the injured trunk,
reckless chop,
What lumber jack did that?

Awe-struck, I watch the tree glow, reflect
silver stars, I anticipate . . .
next swooping fall. I withdraw
to nurse
the tree back to standing life,
shattered Christmas on the floor.

Earthquake in Thessaly

Far from home,
morning journey into Thessaly's
valleys and rugged hills.
I run, dance,
in a trance.
Firs hold my hands, embrace me.

Muses in a chorus, repeat:
a Greek tragedy, syllables rise.

Earth moves at my feet.
Ground cracks. And opens.
Like a jaw
displaying its teeth.

Tremor beneath me, pulls my body
downwards. My screams unheard,
fall of rocks, rip of soil
breaking branches.

My voice, buried.

Silence of Childhood

Fear, a child escapes, flees to another,
help sought.[1]
Protected.
Strategies to overcome,
dependence; security.
Possible triumph—over danger.
Child not unlike an adult:
primitive fear.
Situations arise.
Insecure.
Powerless child, alone incapable.
Others offer and compensate,
child's inadequacies, limits.
Risk of pessimism,
anxiety-generated.
Helping hand of endless
attention.
Not master-slave relations.
Creative.
Independent.
Child discovers autonomy,
self-reliance.
Never absolute.

1. Adler, *Individual Psychology*, 224–25.

Loose Tooth

I feel my tooth wiggle, still stuck,
under my annoyed gum,
lower front—endless irritation.
Bleeds—refuses to be uprooted.
My fingers in my mouth . . .
older sister asserts her skills
as professional extractor.
Discovers the solution to remove
a troublesome tooth.

I listen, follow her instructions:
sis' ties a thread she takes from mom's
knitting basket to my tooth.
Tightly secure, my mouth feels attached
to the living room door by a thread
—level of my head—
I stand a few steps away.
Enough thread slack, slightly drops.
She tightens, measures, tests.
I wait
for the next move:

      door slams shut . . . !

Deep in the Well

Demeter steals the iron sword
from Cadmus
while hunting deer in Thebes.
From the jagged rocks, deadly dragon
blows sulphur and fire,
mortal poison.
She slays the marked beast
with all her force.
Ripping out his teeth, she sews
the yellowed stones into the soil.
She follows Ares our older brother
to the Oracle of Delphi.
Instructions delivered:
dragon teeth for a warrior.
I wake up from my beastly dream
having slept by the well.
Zeus asks Ares to dig deep
into the Theban soil for water.
On the surface of still reflection, a tooth
appears, then sinks,
into the depths of darkness.

Family Ties

Relations serve to express true feelings,
happiness/sadness lived.[1]
Communion growing,
parents/siblings.
Pretence of performance
offers high-class entertainment
to those who know best—*or do they?*
Why the facade?
Common illusion fosters
distractions to relations.
Break defence-mechanism!
Begin by listening: the other.
And what is felt—feeling that way.
To know who I am:
life-time vocation.
Call from within/without—
        order in the universe
        prevails—
        nature instructs.

---

1. Rogers, *Becoming a Person*, 323–24.

Alone at a Table

Eldest cousin marries first, testifies:
woman of conviction.
Little boy, he carries gold rings on a white laced
cushion,
faithfully follows her trail to the reception hall,
not far from Oxford Street.

Congested room of engaged faces
—laughter and chatter.
Queue from party to tables,
meandering bodies,
a lost five-year-old. Uncle instructs
the docile child:
—relocated—which chair to take
at the end
        of a table.
        Boy sits far from his family.
Unknown women model jewellery
in crimson red smiles.
Tobacco smokes rises from lips of bearded men
surveying
imagined performances.

        The boy squeezes in.

Banquet of the Gods

Gold satin tables trimmed
in Athenian lace,
red grapes from the Aegean and Macedon,
decorate the surface.
Lamb cut into quarters, roasted,
spread on bronze platters carved
into vines. Tables display
orange pyramids.
Zeus positions himself at the head.
Men join him, Hephaistos, Ares, Hermes, Dionysios
—even Poseidon, his brother.
Women assemble separated,
Hestia, Hera, Demeter, Clymene and others.
Led to the table with oranges, I stare
at the balanced pyramids from the edge.
Marble terrace splashes
from the shore. Nereids join me.
I glance at Zeus,
struck by his thundering voice.

He carries on. Solemn proclamations.

Dinner without Compeers

Child shifts, authoritarian rule—
asymmetrical adult relations—to peers.[1]
Play friends or imagined.
Time for co-operation presence of likeness
—mates:
    compete . . .
    negotiate . . .
    compromise . . .
"Juvenile era" of resemblance.
How is the child prepared?
    without empathy?
    in harshness?
Alternatives sought:
      sports and music
      competition, creativity
      child co-operates
or discovers—dependence.

1. Sullivan, *Modern Psychiatry*, 38.

Overnight at the Neighbors

Across the busy intersection—
just off Oxford Street
neighbors occupied a two-story house.
Arrangements the boy overhears,
wedding reception . . . sleep overnight
with his family not far away.
The four-year-old vaguely knows them.
Connected somehow to the widow at the corner
—her summer golden gardens.
Perhaps somebody's godparents.
Acquainted with the boy and girl his own age,
play-mates, he thought.
He sleeps in his own bed—brother and sister
bunk together . . .
Then wakes to the voices of mamma and papa,
whispering . . .
They returned to pick him up! As promised!
But they do not approach his bed
or enter the room.
Words fade. Door shuts . . .

Under the Stars

Hestia brings Apollo
to her brother Ares. She proceeds
to Delphi
secure with white-winged Pegasus.
There the women assemble
—days of silence: One.
Hestia provides her chaste wisdom,
discourse for her skeptical
sisters tormented by unruly
husbands.
Wondering about her son Apollo,
her brother Ares assures her Apollo
sleeps safe, untouched...
Apollo lies under the stars
waiting for mother to bring him home.
Ares does not permit Apollo to leave
alone . . .
following mother's orders,
Apollo listens.

Poppy tasted between Apollo's fingers,
he falls asleep.

Misreading Disapproval

Books, loud and soft words,
educating the child—stories—relations.
Tears to strengthen,
not always "disapproval."
"Empathetic linkage"?[1] Child feels
suffocated on a wet pillow.
Flip through pages of emotions
and connect the black and white
paragraphs.
Between the walls
whispers, remarks . . .
grown-up conversations—decisions—
conclusions. To decipher codes:
sounds made symbols, *disapproval*
mistaken.
Child and anxiety squeeze
small sweaty hands.

1. Sullivan, *Modern Psychiatry,* 20–21.

Sleeping at My Grandparents

Papa works fixing cars, family
and neighbors.
Night shift in town.
Mamma and sis' visit family
for the summer—across the Atlantic.
I am a fifteen-minute walk from Oxford Street,
at my grandparents' home.
Red rhododendron burst in corners.
Under twisting canopy of grape vines
I listen to grandpa sing.
Sun sets late, rays massage my
face—ears—neck—arms.
Grandma calls me to bed.
But how can I sleep in one room
without a bed for me?
And so grandpa takes a hammer,
nails, mahogany wood,
and makes me a bed my size,
placed beside theirs.
Heavy cotton blanket crocheted
in blue, green, purple petals.

We sleep like three bears—
          in summer hibernating.

Mighty Kronos Visits

Mother believes I left with father
and Dionysios to the hills
south of Heraklion.
Her mind attentive to the muses—and us.
Or, to taste the purple grapes.
Father understood mother brought
me to Delphi to hear the Oracles.

I remain alone, deserted
—until mighty Kronos arrives!

He inquires about Zeus and Hera.
I sadly explain.
Kronos makes me an arch from birch wood
and demonstrates how to shoot
with the sharp wooden arrow.
Kronos holds the arch and nocks the string,
stands close,
guiding my finger—and release.

The arrow shoots into flight
pierces the sky
and disappears among the gods.

Deficiency Healed

Human deficit
        —made for love—unsatisfied.[1]
Empty: Hole:
    unfulfilled: unrealized:
"love poured"—healing.
        Not exterior—
        nor Cosmetic.
            But interior.
Love "available at the right time."
Not waiting until crisis or trauma
        or adolescence confusion
        or lover's quarrel.
Infant cries out:
        human "love hunger"
            —greatest hunger
to be satisfied
by mortals and the Divine:
            "receive" love
            "give" love.
Difference between rich disinterested B-Love
and selfish, possessive D-love:
        humans need help
        to resolve childhood.

1. Maslow, *Psychology of Being*, 41.

Killing the Devil

Grandma and grandpa's house—
a short distance from Oxford Street—
or a tiresome walk of seven blocks
busy intersection
north one block
to Oxford
and one block west.
Grandpa devoted
to his flower and vegetable gardens.
I keep grandma company.
Daily requirements:
mid-morning beaten eggs with sugar,
nap in the afternoon—
even if I do not feel tired.
But on certain days grandma leaves me behind.
Though I want to accompany her,
she refuses, explains she has a mission
to "kill the devil." I insist with hope
to witness grandma battling that frightful creature:
bat ears, and fangs, and wings,
tail curls into a trident.
I succeed in joining her off to battle,
and endure the afternoon spent chatting
with a shop keeper as grandma purchases
groceries. Waiting, I ask the shop owner,
Is this where the Devil lives?

Movements of the Abyss

I throw rocks into the breathing sea
as if each granite chunk
devoured
by the foaming jaw—unreachable abyss.
Calm waters tease—seduce and deceive.
Poseidon recoils.

Unknown depths:
incertitude and doubt, victims.
Mother speaks of Typhon's power.
She warns me of his frightful evil,
child of Gaius and Tartarus.
My eyes fixed on Ocean; I wonder how father
succeeded in banishing Typhon.

Massive waves crash
on the jagged Aegean coastline.
My body drips:

    Typhon's advance.

Archaic Thoughts

Our thought processes
not any different from "primitive man"—
assumptions differ.[1]
Human nature—*is*:
mind and body: intellect/sense/instincts.
Nothing changes.
Understanding does.
Reason informs us: cause contains
naturalness and perceptibility.
Rational world Graeco-Roman
includes metaphysical,
non-observable, non-material reality,
demarcating framework.
We leave dark forces to the arbitrary—
random unexpected bolt of evil.
Underlying power, causal explanation
dismissed.
Depths of darkness—distance from sun:
evil engenders evil.
To stand above: transcend nature:

drawn or pulled—by light.

1. Jung, *Modern Man*, 125.

My Uncle's Buick

Summer days feel sweaty, long
at my grandparents' home, some blocks away
from Oxford Street. But my uncle
keeps me company—a carpenter
in the day—I never found out where.
Our breezy dinners, windows open
into the sundeck we hear music
of the ice cream truck.
He dashes out to stop the orange
and purple truck to buy me an ice cream.
Chocolate and vanilla cone in my hand,
I eat a nursery rhyme melody.
His toffee Buick I recall:
accompanying him to the drive way
eager to join him, he backs up
without me, and pulls out. He drives
down the block westbound. I follow
him running, until I only touch
red car lights . . .

Aegean Grapes

At dawn mother departs
with Demeter.
Ares replaces her at home.
Father and Dionysios I hear
continue to patrol the eastern
mountains, suspecting another
Titan intrusion. Father argues
the hekatonkheires
demonstrate power
but lack strategy—or do they need it?
I wonder if Ares will remain
to keep me company or respond
to "attacks" in Thessaly.
Boetian hills overlook the Aegean
shores. We hike beneath the sacred
Mount Helicon where muses chant,
we search for honeycomb.
Uncle lets me taste:
he works thick sticky cone
into honey. I dip purple grapes . . .

Tasting Dissatisfaction

Desperate for affection—love,
story of a child-adolescent-adult:[1]
humanness acknowledged:
to Love/Be loved.
Possessed love betrays.
Bumpy road, meanders into valleys
of torment and crests
of unfulfillment.
Ungratified, endless strive, hunger,
thirst—alone. "Ultimate value":
end-goal, return to Aristotle's good life
produces Nicomachean delight.
Goals in small ascents, turns, descents
connected by endless desire,
force to drive around pot holes,
pouring rain, breathing beauty
of evergreen and blue shores
without changing course. Peaks
strengthen—and tempt. To become
who we are:
flourishing, we transcend.

1. Maslow, *Psychology of Being,* 118.

Merry-Go-Round

I joined others, wet from swimming
afternoon in the ocean, my scrawny
kid's body, wet seaweed shorts,
tanned from runs and jumps
on tough logs
rough rocks,
and stops to pat tongue-hanging dogs.
.

Ocean's invitation to seashore
splashes, I throw pebbles,
wait for ripples.

Buzz of green, bees, flies, and mosquitoes,
summer's weapons.
Hum of a low sea-plane,
I wave—imagine my departure.

The Merry-Go-Round turns slow.
I jump on; it speeds and spins.
Dizzy my head, sick my stomach,
I lose control and fly off, hard
landing rolling flat on the ground.

My uncle picks me up,
rubs the bump on my forehead

       head spinning . . .

Strawberry and Pistachios

Scent of cedar, pistachio shades
strawberry trees, ascending
I hear my breath.
Hera's brother, Hermes, stands
ahead of me, like one of the pines.
I taste thistles.
His Olympian trek, smites his spear,
hunting for deer—wild stories
about lion and bear.
Hermes disappears in the morning fog,
rising mist . . .
I remove my muddy sandals,
preferring to run down fields
of wet moss,
delicious Grecian laurel.
Green water falls on polished rocks,
my white chiton wet.
I drink, my lips cooled.
His voice at a distance, his wings mangled
I turn, slip, fall. I hear a robin's cry.
Blue sky descends over me.

Something Like the Gods

Does the child run aimlessly,
driven without a goal?[1]
Or is the little one object-oriented?
Environment, response
to child's creation.
Happiness leads reason, aiming to seek
fulfillment in creativity.
Reflective child pursues the noble,
or the energetic, the beautiful.
Awe-some realization.
    Individual/Unity
    original fashioned.
Child draws the painting
    to be
    to become.
Self empowered to shape person-*ality:*
      teleologically-driven
      "the mover is always the self."
Aristotle disagrees, of course:
    the Unmoved Mover
    moves.
And *Seelenleben,*[2] who moves spiritual life?
But of course, we are like the gods!

1. Adler, *Individual Psychology,* 176–78.
2. *Seelenleben/"spiritual life"*

Dog Named Rex

Autumn pours thistles on leafy tracks
scent of wet bark, treetops spire
into misty clouds.
Thumps approach, paws race
through a bush
black and white Rex halts.
His tongue hangs. He observes:
head low, snout raised,
eyes down, my uncle, his master.
Prized stick in his hand,
Rex jumps
at uncle's raised arm—he throws,
Rex sprints. Eagerly hunts.
Claims the earth—his haven shared
with his master.
Uncle continues the stroll.
Rex vanishes in his search.
Explains the northwest forest,
pacific pines on a twig.
Rex returns
stick firm between his teeth.

Laelaps and Fox Scent

I accompanied Hera's brother.
Ares brought me
to the Boetian fields.
On his hunting expeditions—
he invites me.
Drawing with a stick on the wet soil
the Aegean coastline, the Gulf of Corinth,
solid our position, rough terrain.
Laelaps, plays with Ares,
Zeus' hunting dog.
She sniffs the muddy ground,
storms left their mark,
. . . and fox scent.
Chestnut coat of fur, elegant snout
her ears gracious,
flap on both sides of her head.
Ares' bear hunt depends on Laelaps.
Sleek creature planned to out smart
the red fox, hiding.

Dog Plays Chess without Me

We have numerous opportunities
to "identify"—*ourselves.*[1]
Habits, instruction, encounter
with the world:
son and father—or uncle,
mother and daughter—or aunt,
we determine a meaningful model.
Not every person is qualified as my mentor.
How do I decide?
Crisis means *radical move.*
We are drawn
to the socially meaningful. Child figures
s/he meets the requirements.
Is this even possible?
Or does the mother or father
make the selection? Synthesis
of experience, encounter:
> visual seeks the illumination;
> contemplative attains *theion.*[2]
Hierarchy: best to worst/worst to best—
> now choose.

1. Erikson, *Childhood and Society,* 215.
2. *theion/*"god"

Fishing with My Uncle

Cold—dark—I hear
uncle's voice, green fishing boat
in the garage
attached to the pick-up.
Shore breathes in rhythmic silence.
I put my life jacket on,
we push the boat into the ocean.
Bouncing on waves, he pulls
the throttle. Splashing waters,
he speeds into a void. Engine is off.
Stillness.
Uncle casts a fishing rod
and hands it over to me. He holds
another. Waves bang the boat
like intruding hands.
Stars withdraw yield to orange dawn.
Pastel strokes brush the horizon—
sun blinks purple blue. Rod bends—
tight line, fatigue keeps me from acting.

Dawn catch reeled in.

Poseidon Surrenders

Hermes remained silent about Poseidon,
the serpent poisoned Zeus.
Father warned us—Poseidon's tactics
accompanied by father's rage.
Poseidon lives deep in the ocean
with oceanid friends.
He surfaces with Clymene
to battle, to bite.

News about their wars,
but I never witnessed the scenes.
Each used their lethal weapons.
Wounded Zeus never healed; this I can testify.
Poseidon withdraws to his murky abyss amused,
as if victory for earth and sea.
Poseidon never frightened me—

Uncle Hermes points to the calm ocean waves
reflecting the horizon

where Poseidon might spring out.

Deep Unknown

Experience of anxiety, unknown fears.
Family—
how relationships develop—
without anxiety?
Of being scarred, wounds unhealed.
Hurts. Cuts:
    lifetime to cauterize.
Seek refuge—relief—spiritual ointment.
Human transmission
of red signals—related relations.
Child picks up a new piece of equipment
which we technically call anxiety.[1]
With experience
of pain, and fear, comes a third:
pain you *feel*, I *share.*
Fear repeats:
anxiety remains—shaped outcomes.

1. Sullivan, *Modern Psychiatry,* 19.

Photo on a Horse

On Oxford Street a thin man
wears his plaid shirt, suspenders,
and jeans. Visits our neighborhood
with his horse.

Beautiful smooth brown Saddlebred.
Shiny majestic horse stands
on our green weedy lawn
of dandelion and buttercups.

He hands over a cowboy hat
he helps me put on,
and I grip the sturdy saddle.
I chuckle
at the mounted feeling
so high off the ground.

Photographer
clicks his camera—
without telling me to smile.
My excitement visible
black&white shot—still on the horse,
steady.

    One pose . . .

Whence and Whither

Adler espouses views
of fictional goals,
internal causation—subjective.[1]

Future as present,
"Most important question . . . not whence? But whither?"

Mental constructs
internal—not external determination.

Dispense teleology—
theology for the reigning subject, crowned.

Almost like Humean cause-effect relations,
customs of habit—associations:
    "Whence: From what place?"
    "Whither: To what place?"

Goal of the individual understood:
separate acts—construct a whole.

1. Adler, *Individual Psychology,* 91.

Blue Horizon

Equine shape of the Pegasus
positioned
in the front court.
Doric pillars stand
twining grapevines hang,
clay vases contain orchid
separate green hedges.

I hear the sea, rhythmic splashes
far below, an echo,
along the Athenian shores.

I understand why Pegasus waits;
his wings flap with grace.

Pegasus sketches the open space
into the horizon,
embraced by blue seas and white cloud wisps,
my journey outlined before me.

Place unlike where I live;
my destiny blurry.

Calm caresses me.

Bibliography

Adler, Alfred. *Individual Psychology.* New York: Harper, 1964.

———. *Understanding Human Nature.* London: George Allen, 2010.

Erikson, Erik. *Childhood and Society.* London: Vintage, 1995.

Frankl, Victor. *Man's Search for Meaning.* Boston: Beacon, 2006.

———. *Will to Meaning.* New York: Penguin, 1988.

Freud, Sigmund. *General Introduction to Psychoanalysis.* Hertfordshire: Wordsworth, 2012.

Jung, Karl. *Modern Man in Search of a Soul.* New York: Harcourt, 1933.

Maslow, Abraham. *Towards a Psychology of Being.* Blacksburg: Wilder, 2011.

Rogers, Carl. *On Becoming a Person.* New York: Houghton, 1995.

Sullivan, Harry Stack. *Conceptions of Modern Psychiatry.* New York: Norton, 1953.

www.ingramcontent.com/pod-product-compliance
Lightning Source LLC
Chambersburg PA
CBHW070731030726

47601CB00011B/61